FRANZ SCHUBERT

QUARTET
for 2 Violins, Viola and Violoncello
D minor/d-moll

"Death and the Maiden"
„Der Tod und das Mädchen"

Ernst Eulenburg Ltd
London · Mainz · New York · Paris · Tokyo · Zürich

I.	Allegro	1
II.	Andante con moto	20
III.	Scherzo. Allegro molto	32
IV.	Presto	36

All rights reserved. No part of this publication may be reproduced, stored in a retrieval system, or transmitted in any form or by any means, electronic, mechanical, photocopying, recording or otherwise, without the prior written permission of Ernst Eulenburg Ltd., 48 Great Marlborough Street, London W1V 2BN.

Quartet
I.

Scherzo. Allegro molto.

III.

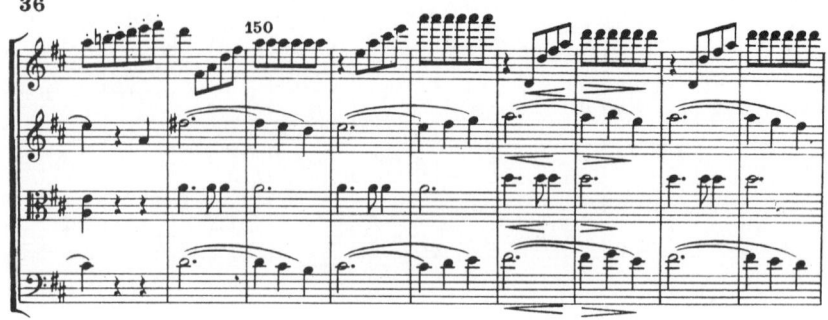

IV.

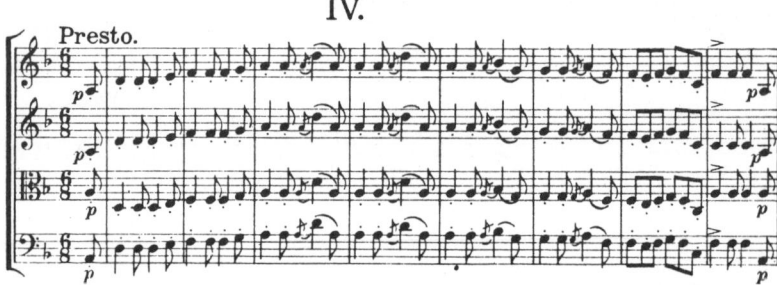

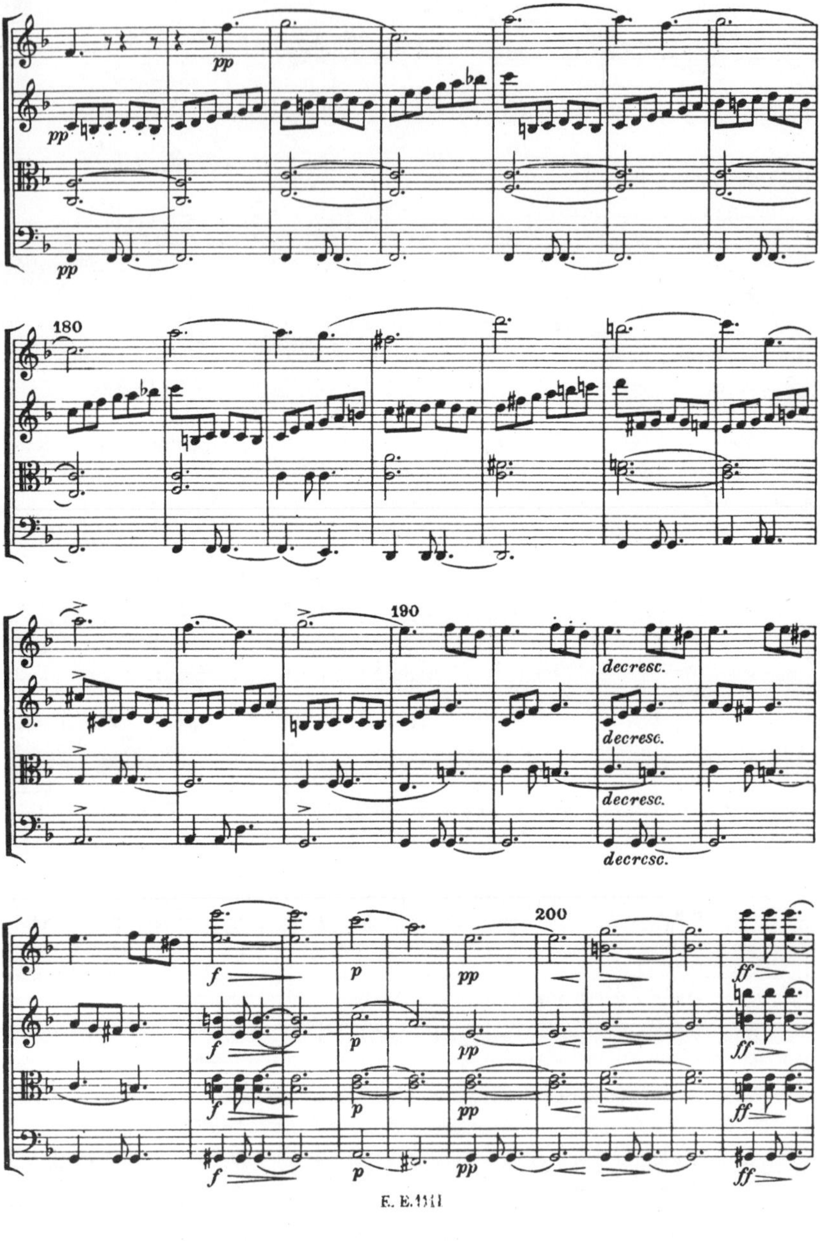
pp
180
190
decresc.
200
f
p
ff

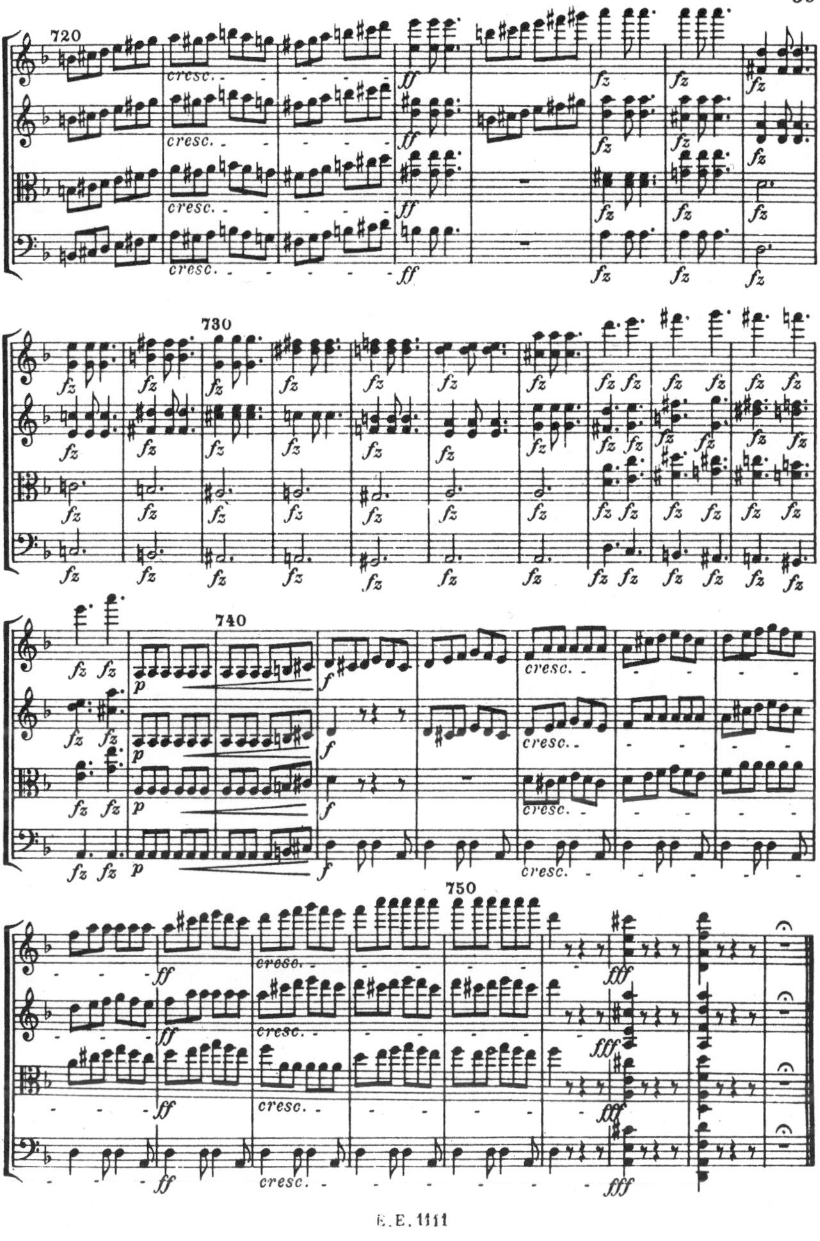
720
cresc.
ff
fz
730
740
p
f
750
fff